Race to Finish

Published in Canada by Millennium Marketing
Saskatoon, SK.
For more information, contact:
marion.mutala@gmail.com
www.babasbabushka.ca

Book design and editing by Kay Petryk, Little Details Editing

Cover design and illustrations by Kevin Peeace
Original cover art: Residential Schools to Reconciliation, 2017
University of Alberta, Coutts Library
Edmonton, Alberta

Author photo by Martin Hryniuk

ISBN 978-1-7773713-1-9 (paperback)
ISBN 978-17773713-2-6 (ebook)

Published in Canada

A portion of the proceeds go to Missing and Murdered Indigenous Women and Girls.

Other Books by Marion Mutala

Children's Books

Baba's Babushka: A Magical Ukrainian Christmas
Baba's Babushka: A Magical Ukrainian Easter
Baba's Babushka: A Magical Ukrainian Wedding
Kohkum's Babushka: A Magical Métis/Ukrainian Tale
Baba's Babushka: A Magical Ukrainian Journey
Baba's Babushka: Magical Ukrainian Adventures
Grateful
More Babas, Please!
My Buddy, Dido!

Poetry

Ukrainian Daughter's Dance

Fiction

The Time for Peace Is Now
Earth Angels: Operation Angel
The Mechanic's Wife
My Dearest Dido: The Holodomor Story
Live Well: My Ukrainian Upbringing and Other Stories
Coming Soon: Baba Sophie's Ukrainian Cookbook

Dedication

One death is one death too many!

When the Covid-19 pandemic hit in early 2020, we soon discovered that was just the tip of the iceberg. This poetry book, *Race to Finish*, is dedicated to all the missing and murdered Indigenous women and girls and to the 215 missing children whose final resting place is Tk'emlúps te Secwépemc, Kamloops Indian Residential School (1860-1969). We honour these children and their families. It is estimated more than 150,000 children attended residential schools in Canada from the 1830's until the last school closed in 1997. Up to 500 students would have been registered at the Kamloops Indian Residential School, according to the National Centre for Truth and Reconciliation (NCTR). Those children would have come from First Nations communities across B.C. and beyond[1].

Another shocking discovery of 751 more unmarked graves was found on the site of Marieval Indian Residential School on Cowessess First Nation which operated from 1899 to 1997, located about 165 kilometres east of Regina, SK[2]. And now 160 more graves

---

[1] https://www.cbc.ca/news/canada/british-columbia/tk-emlúps-te-secwépemc-215-children-former-kamloops-indian-residential-school-1.6043778
[2] https://www.cbc.ca/news/canada/saskatchewan/cowessess-marieval-indian-residential-school-news-1.6078375

found on Penelakut Island, B.C., totalling 1,308 suspected graves and still more expected. We remember and honour you. This is a very tragic part of Canada's history and treatment of Indigenous children, Indigenous peoples and their families.

This book is also to support the Black Lives Matter movement and the many black people who have unjustly lost their lives.

Contents

# Foreword

Written by Kevin L Peeace

I had the opportunity to do class painting projects with students from Wakaw elementary school. I was asked if the Grade 1-3 classes could come and participate in a discussion about myself and my career as an artist. Having answered all their questions, there was a young girl who had a final question. She asked, "What was it like being at the residential school?"

I paused for a few minutes to absorb the gravity of that question. I think it was because I was floored to hear that coming from someone her age or that it caught me totally off guard. In any case, I proceeded to tell the students, "I want you to close your eyes and picture the story in your mind." I continued, "Picture yourself at home, playing and being safe with your parents, it's the end of summer and everything is fine. You hear a knock on the front door, your parents go to open the door and find two people standing there, you can faintly hear the conversation and have no idea what's been said. Reluctantly your parents step aside to let those two strangers come and take you away."

I asked the students about how they felt at this point and what would they plan to do to avoid this situation. Some of their replies were to hide, fight back, run away, or hang onto their parents. I continued the story, "If you tried to hide, they would find you. If you ran away, they would run after you. It was impossible to fight back because, remember, you're only 5-9 years old, so it was easy for the adults to take you. You look to your parents to do something, but they know that if they tried to stop them, they would be charged by the police. The two strangers take you by the arms and lead you into a van. You hear the cries from other children inside the van. Sometimes the last things you saw were the faces of your parents in tears, powerless to help you in your darkest hour."

I then asked the students to open their eyes and they all had looks of shock and sadness, some displayed looks of anger, but mostly disbelief that such a thing could happen. Even as an adult I look back and think how could that have happened to me?

# Never Stop Singing

Does one need a reason to exist?
Does one need a reason to breathe?
Does the sun rise in the east in the morning and
set in the west at night?
Surely, as there is God,
Surely, as there is rain,
Surely, as there are flowers that bloom or
mountains that move,
I will sing.
I will never stop singing.
Black Lives Matter!
Indigenous Lives Matter!

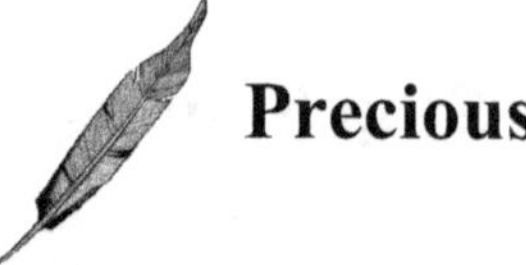 # **Precious**

Many ways to spend a day,
Moments in time are true.
Age increases, time decreases,
Yet, things to say and do.
Days shortened; memories linger.
I still thank God and say
Great blessings of family and special friends.
Plain grateful I am, for today
Few words remain except
it is true.
Precious…
Precious…
You are just precious…
And dear to my heart.

Reminds Me

Reminds me of the old wooden cookstove on the
farm when I was a child on a cold morn.
Reminds me of Old Faithful gushing, ready to
burst.
Or the stars in the sky flickering with love and
delight.
Reminds me of the cross which was hung for all
to see.
Reminds me of…
Your loving touch.

Greatness is Earned

Strive to be great,
The best you can,
To serve, love and achieve
Charity, hope, justice, equality, peace.
Progress towards greatness.
It is said,
"True greatness is earned."
The world has a chance to be genuinely great
With Black and Indigenous protest movements
happening.
People make the world great.

# **Changing**

It is that time
Reflect
A passing moment
Night frost
Changing autumn leaves
Perfect design
Hues radiating
Orange, red, yellow glow
"Only God can make a tree," Kilmer says…
Nature in full blossom positively preserving
Beautifying branches of life
Lungs of the earth
Life-giving rays, changing
Supporting Black and Indigenous lives

 # Freedom

Freedom means a lot to me,
Like to a bird up in the tree.
It flies above the sky so high.
When I see it,
It makes me want to cry.
Because it is free.
I wish it were me.

Freedom means a lot to me,
Like the waves upon the sea.
They roll along the shore so low.
When I see them, they make me want to drift
away.
Because they are free.
Why can't it be me?

Tied to this old life, you know
I will never be free anywhere I go.
I move along each day through.
It makes me sad,
But I know it is true
I will never be free
Like a bird in the tree
Or the waves on the sea.

God's Tricks

Part One

God plays tricks.
Can you not see God laughing?
At birth, we enter the world crying, kicking,
screaming to be heard.
As a baby, life smells good.
With soft, supple skin, our limbs are flexible.
Hungry, we are fed, nourished, and extremely
loved.
We cling to life, receive friendship and human
contact.
Our spirit drives us to survive, and our needs are
met.
Growing, we enter childhood,
Eager, excited, and aware.
Curious and keen to learn,
We start school.
The world is ours to conquer.
Life feels good.

Suddenly, life happens.
Knock one, knock two, and three strikes.
A little of this and a lot of that and too soon
We are in high school dragging our butts around,
Tired, wanting to sleep the days away and party
the nights.
We exist and survive.
Sometimes life feels good and sometimes we are
shown love.
Perhaps secondary school or work,

Marriage, children, sickness, pain,
Joy, and sporadic love.
Some ups and many downs.
Our spirit fights
But our flesh takes over.
At times we are loved and possibly life is good
in return.
God is still laughing,
God is still playing tricks.

For one day,
In the mirror
No longer a child-like face.
We see another wrinkle.
Applying our makeup, we cover our
disfigurements, veins, and warts.
We look old and tired.
We feel defeated.
Unwilling to cope,
Our spirit is fried like a parched desert.

Reborn

Part Two

The second half of our journey begins,
A senior full of wisdom and knowledge.
Few people acknowledge our existence.
Lacking beauty but with much courage.
Strong spiritually, yet physically disabled.
Great energy and desire but no will to carry it
through.
We fight to survive and love deeply
But receive neither recognition nor love in
return.
Caring,
Yet people too busy to notice.
Our age tears at our soul.
We strive to belong and survive
But it is too hard physically.
The pain reminds us that we are almost dead,
Yet, we long to live again
To reminisce about our youth,
To stay alive, to matter.

The Second Coming

Part Three

A strong desire awakens within.
We smile because we know the one who laughs
loves us enormously.
We leave with a grin on our face knowing that it
is all right to laugh, as laughter heals.
And that God tricks us to stay alive, to live life,
to love again.
Finally, we understand.

Don't You Think?

I think if you stand in front of a church with a Bible held high in your hand, you should open it.

I think if you stand in front of a church with a Bible held high in your hand, you should open it and read it.

I think if you stand in front of a church with a Bible held high in your hand, you should open it and read it and turn to 1 Corinthians 13:4-8.

I think if you stand in front of a church with a Bible held high in your hand, you should open it and read it and turn to 1 Corinthians 13:4-8 and see what it says.

I think if you stand in front of a church with a Bible held high in your hand, you should open it and read it and turn to 1 Corinthians 13:4-8 and see what it says and share it with the world.

I think if you stand in front of a church with a Bible held high in your hand, you should open it and read it and turn to 1 Corinthians 13:4-8 and see what it says and share it with the world and use those words in your life.

I think if you stand in front of a church with a Bible held high in your hand, you should open it and read it and turn to 1 Corinthians 13:4-8 and see what it says and share it with the world and use those words in your life daily.

Don't you think?

# **Plain Lucky**

Saunters in like a big teddy bear and gives me a
bear hug.
Certain shyness in his step like dragging feet.
"Hey babe, how's it going?"
How tall was he?
6 feet something. I forget, or did I ever ask?
"New glasses," I say.
"Yeah."
"Cool, looks great."
Always a trendy dresser, intriguing face,
twinkling eyes, smirky smile.
"Coffee with honey and milk?" I ask.
"Sure, thanks."
"Cake?"
"You rock," he says.
"Thanks, hon," so gracious and polite.
"You should read this book."
Hands me the book.
"It's powerful."
"Hey, let's do this book fair or wanna do another
radio interview with Ann Foster?"
"You should definitely come on 'Lit Happens'
again with your new book."
Full of ideas and suggestions.
"I just love your red couch,
Love your place, huge windows, sunshine.
This is just so perfect, peaceful."
Silent for a few moments,
Relaxing, drinking coffee,
Comfortably quiet in each other's company.

How many cups of java did we have together?
"Lunch tomorrow?
11:30, Coachman…" he says.
"Per usual," I say.
Darwin, you are right, he really had a beautiful
quiet side.
I loved that about him.
Unpretentious and real.
Jacquie, so true, so many things we loved.
Lucky.
Yes, plain lucky.
To have known and loved Wesley Donald Funk.

* * * *

*I wrote this poem to read at the late Wes Funk's
funeral and now share it to honour him. Wes
was an activist for 2SLGBTQQIA+.*

# **Envision**

Imagine a clean, green, peaceful city with no crime, no homelessness, everyone fed, clothed, and health care provided, especially for the poor, the less fortunate, and our children.

If all people are looked after, then our whole society does well.

Imagine… people employed, educated, and literate and taking care of each other.

Imagine… utopia… or perhaps Saskatoon.

Why not? If we are going to envision, go big.

Imagine heaven on earth… we are called to care and strive for excellence. Why not envision the best city in Saskatchewan, in Canada, in the entire world?

We have the potential. Our greatest human resource is people. Our youth are educated and shipped to other places. Let us value children, the weak, the poor, the homeless, and those unable to care for themselves. Let us keep people employed, build our cities with high ideals, free education, and medical care.

Build what we envision. It is up to the people of Saskatoon, to demand our leaders to put in programs that support people. Saskatoon can make Black Lives and Indigenous Lives Matter. Saskatoon can become the greatest city on earth.

I envision and I am willing to work for this kind of city.

Are you?

Getting Nowhere Fast

He said he had writer's block.
I asked, "What is that?"
He replied, "You know."
I said, "No, I do not."
"Writer's block."
"You mean a chip off the old block?"
"No.
Being blocked,
Feeling blocked."
"Oh, like the Parti Quebec Bloc
Or the Separatists Bloc."
The Free Dictionary: the temporary inability for
a writer to think of what to write.
"I have writer's block now and cannot seem to
get a sensible sentence on paper."
I remark, "You say."
He responds, "My ideas flowed like gravy, like
ice cream melting in the sun, like honey-sticky
sauce but intense,
Like a blizzardy, snowy day in Saskatchewan,
wild and crazy."
"Did you see a doctor?" I said.
"What for?" he asked.
"A vaccine, a cure
To help you with this condition."
"What condition is that?"
"Writer's block?"
"Why?"
"Have you got a cramp in your hands?" I
inquired.

"Writer's block," he declared emphatically.
"The only thing that is blocking you is your
white attitude.
So, start writing and change,
Because artists are writing and speaking for
change in black and white and all Indigenous
colours.
A huge double helix rainbow delight happening
in the world."

What I Noticed

What I noticed is that love is love and hate is hate and whether you are gay or straight, we are all humans and vulnerable and life is tough – relationship stuff – and the simple fact – we need each other – is true, so being kind is where it's at and that's a fact! Yeah, baby that's a fact, and where it's at. Yes, it is where it's at and definitely that – Amen!

What I noticed is Black and Indigenous Lives Matter!

Suffering

The world is rapidly changing.
Our skies are turning to mud,
The earth gives birth to new resources like a
woman constantly in labour,
Suffering continues…
Suffering continues…

There are groups demanding their rights.
Each wants to be heard.
Committees are formed, letters are sent
Contradicting each other.
People are not unified…
People are not unified…

Investment is high, development low,
Ends are just being met.
Prices rise, profits reaped,
But suffering continues…
Suffering continues…
Still suffering continues…

# Baby Seat

He was driving a black Honda CRV, brand new, 2021, and was wearing a black classic business suit and green tie, white shirt, freshly showered, clean-shaven, handsome dude sporting a leather briefcase and was on his way to work.

He had a baby seat in the backseat, at 7am, and he was on his way to work with his black leather briefcase, clean-shaven and handsome, freshly showered with a classic black business suit and green tie, white shirt and driving his black brand-new Honda CRV 2021.

We dickered on the price, what he wanted, and arguably settled, and I didn't want to but…

I had a baby at home sleeping and needed baby formula.

He had a baby seat in the back, and I had a baby sleeping at home and society says I am the problem.

It was 7 am and he had a baby seat in the backseat.

I Walk with You

Silently slowly, stoically,
Head lowered into the wind.
Frosty air chills
For all the injustices.
All the pain and sorrow felt
For all bad treatment.
Steps never taken.
Yet my soul, my sister spirit,
For all the missing and murdered Indigenous
women and girls,
I walk with you.

 # Silent

I was silent…
silent, about so many things…
silent…
I just let it happen, watching, waiting,
listening…
I was silent…
silent about so many things…
I never spoke up, voiced my opinion, and
expressed my concern…
I was silent…
silent about so many things…
I was afraid, lacked courage, at a loss for
words…
I was silent…
silent about so many things for fear of criticism,
the inability to articulate my visions, my ideas…
I was silent…
silent about so many things…
It was difficult to find the vocabulary; words
escaped me; my mind overwhelmed with
thoughts never uttered from my lips…
I was silent…
silent about so many things in my life…
I could not find my voice, the right side of the
brain that deals with speech blocked, my words
befuddled, the messages scrambled…
I was silent…
silent about so many things, my power taken
away, my voice evaporated, gone…
completely silent…

a mute…
I was silent…
silent… about… so… many… things… until…
now…
I am not silent anymore.

# **White Privilege**

What do I know about being black?
Indigenous?
2SLGBTQQIA+?
I am none of these,
What do I know of systemic racism?
Having never felt it.
I have seen it but never felt it.
Feeling and experiencing,
Two different worlds.
I have created it.
Yes, I am white privileged and have experienced
walking into a store
People accept me.
Blonde hair, blue eyes,
White as the prairie snow.
No one suspects,
No one hurls insults,
No one glares.
They look at me with different eyes.
I have tried to stop racist remarks to my students
when I was teaching from other white privileged
people, I was their protector at school.
But when class is dismissed,
Indigenous and Black children in the world
Need separate tools to survive from us,
White privilege.

# **Colour-Blind**

Beyond
Examine character
Race should not matter
Religion, non-issue
Treat with dignity
Creed and political affiliation should not
interfere with human rights
Equality
Yet, Cain slew Able his brother, and I guess
Two people meet = trouble
Isolation
Or do we need to become colour-blind?

I Cannot Be Silent Anymore

The sin of omission as a Catholic is considered a deadly sin… watching something despicable and not doing anything about it or seeing harm and closing one's eyes to a situation.

I cannot be silent anymore.

Ignorance inexcusable.

The need to speak out to prevent bad things from happening to others.

It is unacceptable to say nothing.

I do not have the strength to do many things, or the financial resources to help, but I do have my voice and the ability to write and speak out loud, to protest.

Therefore, I have a responsibility to lead a discussion and talk about issues like bullying, the persecution of 2SLGBTQQIA+ because of their sexual orientation, racism, sexual exploitation of young innocent children, child pornography, and Black and Indigenous Lives Matter.

Human sex slavery – crime of the 21st century.

We need to address and put laws in place to stop all crimes against humanity,

We need to protect Black and Indigenous lives.

Do not be silent!

Attitudes need to change,

White privilege stopped.

As a woman, a mother, a teacher, an author, an artist, a human being.

What does humanity say about a society that does not speak up?

That exploits the weak and innocent?

I **can** change my white attitude towards the treatment of Black and Indigenous Lives.

There is power in the written word,

But when it is spoken, it is dope.

I cannot be silent anymore.

Can you?

 # Stand Up

Stand up and be counted.
People, stand up,
Be counted for peace.
Stand up and be counted again and again.
If you are against war,
Willing to work for peace,
Willing to find alternatives to resolving conflict
Peacefully,
Stand up,
Be counted
Today.
For future generations,
For expectant mothers who say, "I don't want
my son or daughter to die.
I raised them to live, to love, to dream, and to fly
high."
So, stand up, I say.
Stand up.
Stand up right now,
Be counted and speak up for Blacks and
Indigenous people and 2SLGBTQQIA+ and
#METOO.
Eliminate white privilege and systemic racism.

Speak the Truth

Black and Indigenous lives matter and there is
systematic racism and white privilege
Speak the truth

# Smarten Up

Smarten up people, give your head a shake.

What is happening out there?

But then people would say that Marion is off her rocker,

Marion does not know what she is talking about.

You see, I know they know about white privilege, I know they know what is right when we talk about Black Lives Matter and Indigenous Lives Matter and that systemic racism does exist.

Come on now, people.

What's up?

Perhaps Marion is off her meds talking about this stuff in front of an audience, too. Oh dear, give her some medicinal marijuana to fix her.

She is just using her white privilege. Yes, her white privilege, that is what it is, and yes, she is, and Marion could be off her rocker or on a medicinal compound of some sort.

But it does not take a rocket scientist to know or to notice what is happening now in the world, does it? Right, am I correct?

I am white privileged, so I am talking to the other white privileged.

Smarten up, you know exactly what I mean, stop it.

And sometimes it takes 22 seconds of silence to figure what to say when someone does or says something totally stupid and you are still in shock because that is how I feel about what is happening in the world. Shock and disbelief that in the 21st century we are witnessing numerous murders by cops, when we are trying to send people to Mars, and we have to have #METOO movements and talk about race to try and fix this.

Indigenous and Black Lives Matter so do 2SLGBTQQIA+.

Smarten up people, let's fix this. You know what I am talking about, and no, Marion has never tried medicinal compounds because the world is too crazy for me to start doing that and the world is not ready for Marion on marijuana or any other substance.

Smarten up!

 **215**

What's in a number?
215 pairs of tiny feet
Walking no more.
215 pairs of eyes,
Visions exterminated.
Shall we count them?

215 souls stolen,
lost,
now found
in a graveyard.
Young as 3 years old,
a mere baby taken,
robbed from their parents.
Missing children,
final resting place Tk'emlúps te Secwépemc
Kamloops Indian Residential School (1860-
1969).
215 undocumented deaths.
We honour these children and their families.

# Every Child Matters!

There are no words to describe this Indigenous genocide.

Every child matters!

# **Race to Finish**

Will we make it?
It does not look like it if you watch TV.
But movements are happening and in the right
direction, but we have seen it before with Martin
Luther King, Louis Riel, Nora Bernard, Anne
Cools, Chief Dan George (Tsleil-Waututh),
Alanis Obomsawin (Abenaki), and Drake.
Indigenous Lives Matter.
Black Lives Matter.
So, with time on our side due to the strange
COVID-19 pandemic
slowing down the world, let us evaluate what
really matters.
What do we value?
Lives.
Let us talk about justice, equality, and human
rights.
We have time to stand and be the voice for
change.
Can we race to finish?
Or will race wars finish humanity?

Open Dialogue:
Tell Us your Story

1. What situations have occurred to you regarding systemic racism, racism, bullying, sexual harassment, homophobia, and/or other discrimination?

2. What are things people can do to prevent this from occurring?

3. What are things people can do to promote reconciliation?

4. What are things people can do to promote peace?

5. What are things people can do to prevent racism, systemic or otherwise?

6. What are things people can do to stop bullying or sexual harassment?

7. What are things people can do to stop homophobia?

8. What are things people can do to stop other discrimination?

Tell us your story so we can listen, understand, and change to make life better.

Resources

<u>Health Services</u>

- ➢ **Government of Canada Mental Health Services:** www.canada.ca/en/public-health/services/mental-health-services
- ➢ **Saskatchewan Accessing Health Care Services:** www.saskatchewan.ca/residents/health/accessing-health-care-services

<u>Resources for People Experiencing Violence and Abuse</u>

- ➢ **Women's Shelters Canada:** www.sheltersafe.ca/
- ➢ **Government of Canada Bullying Prevention Programs:** www.canada.ca/en/public-health/services/bullying/bullying-prevention-programs.html
- ➢ **Kids Help Phone:** 1-800-668-6868
- ➢ **Childhelp National Child Abuse 24/7 Hotline (multilingual service available):** 1-800-422-4453
- ➢ **Saskatchewan Human Rights Commission Erasing Racism info sheet:** www.saskatchewanhumanrights.ca/education-resources/information-sheets/erasing-racism/
- ➢ **myPlan Canada App:** https://myplanapp.ca/en/
- ➢ **Canadian Centre to End Human Trafficking Hotline:** 1-833-900-1010

<u>Resources for Indigenous Peoples</u>

- ➢ **The National Residential School Crisis Line:** 1-866-925-4419
- ➢ **National Aboriginal Circle Against Family Violence:** www.nacafv.ca/
- ➢ **Hope for Wellness 24/7 Help Line:** 1-855-242-3310

<u>Resources for 2SLGBTQQIA+</u>

- ➢ **Youthline:** www.youthline.ca/
- ➢ **Egale:** https://egale.ca/

About Marion Mutala

Marion Mutala has a master's degree in educational administration and taught for 30 years. With a passion for the arts, she loves to write, sing, play pickleball and guitar, travel, and read. Marion has written 16 books to date.

She is the author of the National Bestselling, Award-winning children's books, *Baba's Babushka: A Magical Ukrainian Christmas* (Anna Pidruchney Award, 2010), *Baba's Babushka: A Magical Ukrainian Easter* (shortlisted for Saskatchewan Book Award, Publishing in Education, 2013), *Baba's Babushka: A Magical Ukrainian Wedding* (Winner of The High Plains Book Award, Best Children's Book, 2015), and *Kohkum's*

Babushka: A Magical Metis/ Ukrainian Tale. She is also the author of *Grateful, The Time for Peace is Now, Ukrainian Daughter's Dance* (a poetry collection), *The Mechanic's Wife* (Silver Winner, Destiny Publishers Fiction, 2015), *More Babas, Please!, My Buddy, Dido!* (Shortlisted for a High Plains Book Award, Best Children's Book, 2019), and *My Dearest Dido: The Holodomor Story*, a book about the Ukrainian genocide also available in audiobook.

Books released in 2020 include a chapbook called *Earth Angels: Operation Angel* with all sale proceeds donated to Nashi, an organization aimed at stopping human trafficking of children; *The Mechanics Wife* (second edition) on amazon.ca; and her new book in the Baba's collection called *Baba's Babushka: A Magical Ukrainian Journey* is included in a 10th Anniversary Limited Edition Hardcover Book of four stories called *Baba's Babushka: Magical Ukrainian Adventures. Live Well: My Ukrainian Upbringing and Other Stories* was recently released by Hidden Book Press.

Race to Finish is Marion's second book of poetry.

Coming soon: *Baba Sophie's Ukrainian Cookbook*

Website: www.babasbabushka.ca
Twitter @Babamarion
www.facebook.com/marion.mutala

 # About the Artist

Kevin L Peeace was born in 1972 in Kelvington, Saskatchewan. He is a member of Yellowquill First Nations (Saulteaux) and Peter Chapman First Nations (Cree). Kevin is a survivor of the Indian Residential School system having attended both Gordon's near Punnichy and St. Michaels in Duck Lake for six years in his early childhood. In 1985, his late mother Ann Whitehead moved the family out to B.C., eventually settling in Mission. In 1991, he graduated from Mission Secondary School, soon after enrolling at UCFV – Abbotsford in the Studio Fine Arts Diploma Program and successfully completing it in 1993. He moved to Vancouver that year, continuing his studies at Capilano College in North Vancouver where he pursued studies in Fine Arts, History, Anthropology, and Archaeology.

In 1995, Kevin entered his professional career in art under the guidance of his uncle Jerry Whitehead. In the summer of that year, he returned to his roots in Saskatchewan and continued pursuing his goal of becoming an artist.

Fast forward 22 years later, he has discovered many things in his life that art has brought, most importantly the love of a great wife Vicki Head, his three beautiful children, Dawn, Eve, and Raymond, and two grandchildren, Daniel and Raven. The importance of family is the central core of his paintings: they are tributes to all the great women in his life who've made significant contributions to his existence, and they remind him of the past we share and of the future of his children. Kevin is proud to represent his people through art; it is a blessing to be given these gifts and equally to share with people all over the world. It is his wish that his paintings will inspire our children to give hope, to be positive, and to always strive to reach their dreams.